"ON THE MOVE"
Views of Transport in
Barking and Dagenham 1890 – 19͜͜

Compiled by:
Susan Curtis

LIBRARIES DEPARTMENT

1993
LIBRARIES DEPARTMENT
LONDON BOROUGH OF BARKING AND DAGENHAM

CONTENTS

Cover Photograph:
Horse-drawn hand pump used by Barking Town Firemen in the late 19th Century.

DEDICATION

This volume is dedicated to the memory of James Howson, former Curator/Archivist at Valence House Museum. He died in August 1993 aged 71.

Jim worked extremely hard to build up and document a collection of archival photographs. The Libraries Department is now able to reap the benefit of his labour and produce lavishly illustrated local history publications for educational purposes.

INTRODUCTION

In the years between 1890 and 1959, Barking and Dagenham developed from a predominantly rural part of Essex into an industrial and residential suburb of England's capital city.

A dominant influence in this radical change was the parallel landmarks in the advances of transport and communications.

This book aims to illustrate transport throughout seventy years of Barking and Dagenham's history. Photographs are shown in chronological order, with a brief introduction highlighting major innovations and events recorded in each decade.

This is possible due to the richness of the photographic collections housed at Valence House Museum, Dagenham, Essex.

Thames Sailing Barges trapped in the ice at a frozen Barking Creek in February 1895.

At the close of the 19th century, air transport was limited to hot-air balloons, gliders and airships.
The second Boer War took place in South Africa from 1899 to 1902, following the first Boer War (1880 – 1).

In the late 19th century, Barking and Dagenham was still predominantly rural. This idyllic view of the leafy Upney Lane shows a horse and carriage taking a leisurely break.

In 1894, before motorised transport and electricity in Barking, these oil lamp attendants used hand carts accompanied by the occasional dog.

A visit to Rookery Farm, Dagenham by officials from West Ham County Borough Council, *circa* 1894, This farm was purchased by West Ham to provide a smallpox isolation hospital, It later became Dagenham Hospital, which closed in 1986. The party pose in front of an impressive carriage drawn by two horses.

The brigade rush out from Barking Fire Station in East Street, driving a horse-drawn appliance.

When Dagenham Dock was being developed by Samuel Williams in the late 19th century, the only ready-made facility was a rusty line of rails leading to the main railway. This picture shows No. 2 of four Manning Wardle locomotives purchased from contractors who had recently constructed Tilbury Docks, *circa* 1897.

Traffic on the River Thames at Dagenham *circa* 1897. In the foreground is a steam tug used by Samuel Williams & Sons at Dagenham Dock. It had 2 cylinders and was built by John Dudgeon of Cubitt Town in 1875.

Thames Sailing Barges moored at "The Mill Pool" in Barking, *circa* 1899.

The Handley Page Type D Monoplane.

In 1903, two inventors called Wilbur and Orville Wright flew a heavier-than-air machine over the beach at Kitty Hawk, North Carolina.

In 1909, the Frenchman Louis Blériot became the first man to successfully fly over the English Channel.

Chadwell Heath Railway Station, which opened in 1864, seen before the turn of the century.

William French, Station Master, with his family outside his house at Dagenham East Railway Station, *circa* 1900. This station opened in 1885, when the London, Tilbury and Southend Railway opened as far as Upminster. In 1932, two new electrified tracks extended from Barking and Dagenham East was rebuilt as a District Line halt.

Barking Railway Station, *circa* 1900, viewed from the level crossing at the east end, before widening took place.

AN OUTING LEAVING CHADWELL HEATH.

A "Band of Hope" party pictured outside Grove Farm, Chadwell Heath, *circa* 1900.

Mrs. Jane Flint and her family with a Poulter's Dairy milk wagon outside her farm in Halbutt Street, Dagenham, *circa* 1903. Note the milkman serves from his churn by using a jug.

Barking Council fire-fighting vehicle and the team commanded by Chief Officer Galloway (on the left). Compare with photograph number 5.

Works outing from Dagenham Dock to Theydon Bois, *circa* 1906.

THE NEW STATION AT BARKING.

The new station at Barking seen from the Forest Gate Down platform in 1908.

Frederick Handley Page, a notable pioneer of flight, seen with an experimental glider in 1908. The Handley Page works in Creekmouth, Barking was the first British factory exclusively constructed for the manufacture of aircraft in 1909.

In 1909, the Royal Aeronautical Society of Great Britain selected land at Dagenham Breach as the site for it's Experimental Flying Ground. On the left, Major B.F.S. Baden-Powell (brother of the Chief Scout and past president of the Society) is seen with the Australian, A.J. Roberts in front of C.A. Moreing's Voisin Biplane.

Various decorated vehicles take part in the Dagenham Carnival Procession, past the Parish Church of St. Peter and St. Paul, in 1912.

In 1913, the mass production of motor cars was introduced by Henry Ford in Michigan, U.S.A. He aimed to produce 250,000 Model T cars in 1914 using a moving assembly line.

The decade, however, was dominated by the dramatic events shaping World War I (1914-1918). The "tank" was developed in secrecy, and infantrymen took part in the "Battle of the Somme" using this new weapon.

Francis Healey, an Australian engineer who invented radio control for pilotless aircraft, torpedoes and airships, seen at the Dagenham Flying Ground. In the hangar is the engine and propeller of his radio-controlled airship.

Healey (on the right) pictured with a Royal Engineers team inflating his new airship at Dagenham Experimental Flying Ground.

High Road, Chadwell.

Looking west along High Road, Chadwell Heath, *circa* 1910. The tram line from Ilford to Chadwell Heath had officially opened on 14th March 1903. Notice the single-track section near The Greyhound public house on the right.

Wagon and trailer used by Leftley's of Heath Street, Barking to transport flour. The wagon was fuelled by a coal fired boiler and could carry 6 tons of freight.

Barking Urban District Council first opened a tramway in 1903. Car No. 1 is pictured here, advertising local shops.

Mr. Holmes is seen with the first motor van used by Barking Urban District Council's Electricity Department in 1912.

Produce of James Alfred Parrish of Hearn Farm, Dagenham, which was situated near the Three Travellers public house on Beacontree Heath, loaded onto wooden farm wagons.

The Handley Page "Yellow Peril" monoplane of 1911 outside the factory at Creekmouth, Barking.

This Barking Tramcar was wrecked at Jenkins Lane during a gale on 27th December 1913.

An outing from The Harrow public house at Ripple Road, Barking, *circa* 1919.

From 1901 to *circa* 1923 land on the Parsloes Estate was used by the National Trotting Horse Breeders Association. Pony-trotting competitions were held at the race track. This picture shows the stable blocks, *circa* 1919.

A motor car with the registration number XX3420 passing through East Street, Barking in 1923.

Popular motoring boomed after the end of the Great War in 1914. In May 1923 the first twenty four hour Grand Prix motor car race took place.

Farm wagons parked outside the barn at Lakes Farm, Dagenham, *circa* 1920.

This busy scene in the Broadway, Barking, features a No. 1 open-top tramcar destined for Beckton and a "Route 67" vehicle travelling to Aldgate, *circa* 1921.

General omnibus "NS 905" type vehicle destined for Marylebone Station bearing a 1923 registration number.

A Royal party visited Ilford, the Becontree Housing Estate and Barking on 12th June 1923. The throng at Blakes Corner, Barking wave to the vehicles.

A Barking Baptist Tabernacle Horse-brake excursion, *circa* 1923, The Reverend and Mrs. Taylor can be seen on the front seat.

Barking Council Electricity Department take a char-a-banc outing to Southend in 1925.

THE BOTTLE-NECK AT "THE ANGLERS' RETREAT" ON THE MAIN LONDON ROAD, WHICH THE DAGENHAM URBAN DISTRICT COUNCIL WISH TO WIDEN. (11)

Traffic congestion in the 1920's. This shows the bottle-neck at The Anglers' Retreat public house in New Road, Dagenham, *circa* 1926. The Urban District Council planned to widen this road to ease the situation.

The Becontree Estate Railway, *circa* 1927. The building contractors constructed a supply railway to undertake the task of moving building materials. Here the engine "Dagenham" is seen between The Chequers public house and Gale Street.

Char-a-banc convoy carrying participants in the "Barking's Beautiful Babies" special event which celebrated National Baby Week in 1927.

East Street, Barking, *circa* 1928. In the centre, tramcar No. 1 is destined for Chadwell Heath. It is overtaking a small delivery van advertising "Carr's biscuits" which is parked outside Arthy's cake shop. On the left is a horse-drawn cart bearing the name of I. Leftley, transport contractor.

Beckton Tram Depot, 1928. Looking back towards Barking from the end of the line, over Barking tramcars No. 1 and 2.

Tramcar No. 3 crossing the Bascule Bridge, Barking on 13th October 1928. The bridge was built in 1903 in order to transport many Barking residents who were employed at the Beckton Gas works. The tram service was withdrawn in 1929 and the bridge, which contained over 600 tons of iron and steel, was broken up for scrap.

"General" omnibus number 148 crossing Dagenham Heathway Bridge in 1929, en route to The Chequers public house.

Chadwell Heath High Road, circa 1935.

In 1931, the production of motor vehicles commenced at the Ford Motor Company works in Dagenham.
1934 saw the launch of the famous liner "The Queen Mary". She was the most powerful ship in the world at this time. Her maiden voyage to New York began on 27th May 1936. In the following year Britain's first aircraft carrier, The Ark Royal, was built at a cost of £3 million. This decade closed dramatically when Britain declared war on 3rd September 1939.

Chequers Corner. Dagenham.   122669

Tilbury Coaches vehicle, registration number EV2507, bound for East Ham. It has stopped at The Chequers public house (see page 45) which was demolished in the late 1980's.

This 1899 model Daimler car took part in the Dagenham Civic Day procession on 31st January 1931. The aim of the vehicle was to raise funds for the Becontree Annexe of the King George Hospital at Five Elms, Dagenham.

Barking's charter celebrations in October 1931. The famous actress Anna Neagle (on the right) and the Mayoress, Mrs. A. E. Martin, bravely took to the water in Barking Park. The rubber airboat in the picture was an industrial product of the town.

A policeman directs traffic at Blakes Corner, Barking in 1933. Busy traffic conditions can be seen at the junction of Ripple Road, East Street and Linton Road (note the Linton Laundry in the background).

Looking at Barking Broadway from North Street, *circa* 1935. This policeman has little traffic to direct, note tram number 67 in the rear.

Looking northwards at Whalebone Bridge, Chadwell Heath, *circa* 1935. Traffic conditions were congested in the mid-1930's before this road was widened.

A police car parked in Shafter Road. This vehicle was in use at Dagenham Police Station in 1937.

A lorry bearing a concrete breaking machine is seen undertaking roadworks on the Barking by-pass on 30th March 1938.

DCI Aircraft seen at Castlefield, Dagenham in 1938.

Staff pictured with part of Barking's fleet of ambulances, prepared to deal with wartime emergencies, outside the Civil Defence Depot at Cambell School.

The Cunard ship the "Mauretania" passing the Ford Motor Company works at Dagenham on 6th August 1939 at about 6 p.m. This was the only visit this ship made to London. She arrived at King George the Fifth Dock at 7. 30 p.m.

A Wartime Memory
November 1939
A Barrage Balloon at its
moorings

An image from the early days of World War II showing a Barrage Balloon moored at Dagenham Dock.

This emergency food van was built on a Ford 10 horse power chassis. It was provided by the Ford Emergency Food Van Trust to help solve the problem of serving hot food to air raid victims.

A visit to the Ford Motor Company works at Dagenham by the Royal Air Force shows a female mechanic working on the production line.

World War II bomb damage to railway carriages and track at the Dagenham Dock Industrial Estate. The Ford Motor Company works was a prime target for German bombers.

Holes were blasted in the roofs of the radiator and press shops at the Ford Motor Company works. Production of vehicles, however, was continued shortly after damage had occurred.

In the foreground, Home Guard volunteers are seen aboard a Thames Lighter at Dagenham Dock. Two tugs also feature in this wharfside scene during World War II.

The first half of the decade was dominated by World War II. Much of the action involved air transport, e.g. "The Battle of Britain", "The Blitz", "The Dambusters" and the bombing of Dresden. The war ended on 13th May 1945.
In 1948, a U.S. aeroplane called "The Bell", broke the sound barrier for the first time.

Eddie Gillan drives a traditional vehicle for Spurrier's Bakeries of Barking. He is seen delivering bread in Blackbourne Road, Dagenham on 17th October 1940.

Post-war Dagenham pictured in a view to the northern entrance to Dagenham Dock Railway Station in Chequers Lane, 1947.

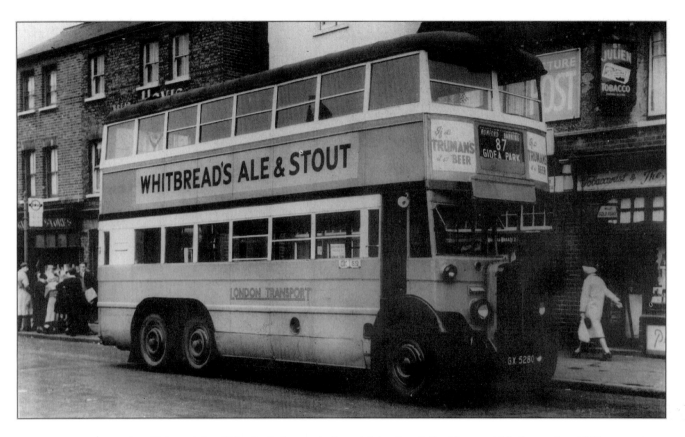

An LT type bus, number 87 bound for Gidea Park, is seen in Longbridge Road, Barking on 11th September 1948.

Dealing with severe winter weather conditions in 1949. Two men are working on the Borough of Dagenham's "Ashbury" gritter in order to make the roads safer.

A Trolleybus seen in East Street, Barking during the 1950's. This "Type SA3" vehicle on route 691 was destined for Barking Broadway.

The modern age of popular motoring for the masses developed in the 1950's. In 1953, car prices fell due to a price war between various manufacturers. The "Ford Popular" costing £390, including tax, was the world's cheapest four-cylinder car.

Horse-drawn milk van delivering bottles of milk to a local school for post-war pupils to drink during their break. The United Dairies vehicle is pictured in Becontree Avenue, Dagenham on 23rd May 1950.

Congested traffic awaits an approaching train at Ripple Road level crossing, Barking on 9th April 1951.

Scene from a pageant in the grounds of Valence House, Dagenham in June 1951. This formed part of the Government sponsored "Festival of Britain" celebrations.

In 1951, Dagenham Committee for Education organised for local children to learn how to cross busy roads safely.

Industrial traffic, mainly consisting of cyclists pictured outside May and Baker's chemical factory in Rainham Road South, Dagenham. Employees are leaving work at 6 p.m. on 15th September 1952.

The Borough of Dagenham's Highways and Works Committee displayed a decorated vehicle in the "Town Show" of 1953.

In 1953 car prices fell dramatically in a cost-cutting war. The worlds cheapest 4-cylinder car costing £390, the Ford Popular, was introduced. Here a queue of vehicles in Valence Avenue wait to buy fuel in Whalebone Lane South during the petrol strike of 1953.

Old tracks for trams are being removed from the centre of East Street, Barking on 29th October 1953.

Looking west from the North Street footbridge, a steam train is leaving Barking Station headed by a Stanier class four two-six-four tank locomotive, in 1955.

Samuel Williams & Sons Road Transport building at Dagenham Dock, June 1955.

A scooter rally formed part of the Dagenham Town Show in 1957. This mode of transport became a prominent feature of members of "mod" gangs in the 1960's.

Traffic in Rainham Road South, Dagenham near The Bull inn, on 21st April 1958. The road was later widened to ease congestion.